A
Meteorologist
in
the
Promised
Land

BECKA MARA MCKAY

A Meteorologist
in the Promised Land

Shearsman Books
Exeter

First published in the United Kingdom in 2010 by
Shearsman Books Ltd
58 Velwell Road
Exeter EX4 4LD

www.shearsman.com

ISBN 978-1-84861-083-5
First Edition

Acknowledgements
Some of the poems in this collection previously appeared as follows:

ACM: 'Seventeen Lessons About Utopia'
American Letters and Commentary: 'TABLOIDS'
Columbia: 'Letters to the Minor Prophet'
Controlled Burn: 'How to Picture an Edge'
Cranky: 'T'Philot' and 'Letter from the Editor'
Hotel Amerika: 'The War in the North: A Report'
Rattapallax: 'Epithalamium', 'Good Excuses in Lousy Weather', and 'A
Meteorologist in the Promised Land'
small spiral notebook: 'The Thesaurus Fails to Replace the Direction of the
Sun', 'You Are Not Here', and 'Birds in April'
Third Coast: 'In Praise of the Overlooked' and 'After the Tombs'.

'Birds in April' was nominated for a 2006 Pushcart Prize.

A grant from the Seattle Arts Commission helped make this book possible.

Cover image, 'Á Bao A Qu (II)' copyright © Brian Booker, 2009.

Contents

The thorn in turn became the means
to lift the leaves off of the ground.
—Andy Goldsworthy

For my mother. Nancy McKay,
and for Fran and Marv Tepper

BIRDS IN APRIL

Birds in April

Except for the imperative *wait here*

    and what rises to the interrogative,

now? when?   the tongues I've learned don't offer word-

    for-word translation. They are glass,   *aim and*

fire   silvered backs scraped clean

    of known intonations.   *really?*   Negotiation

leans a thin shoulder into patience. *repeat, please*   Orders

    and questions, briefest pleas—only these

surrender directly, prepared for grasping   *give*

    without mediation.   *run*   Departing,

the lover suddenly understands all

    the world's languages, *go*   as though platoons

of dictionaries have stormed re-opened

    recesses in his intellect. He leaves

anyway.   *again?*   What remains is

    a space that can't contain him, but which

he will not stop haunting.   *hush*   The killdeer

feigns a broken wing to draw thieves from the nest.

How fierce was I supposed to be? Cardinals

will battle their own reflections in spring.   *how?*

quick, come   No one is looking back at me.

T'philot (Prayers: Jerusalem, summer)

1. *For Vesalius*
Jerusalem is Rome
ecorché. Skinned city
teaching anatomy
in her eyeless tomb.
Peeled, the body reveals
nothing. Tendon
plucked from muscles,
muscles cleaved from bone.

2. *For the Galilee*
The Kinneret cannot roll
like her sister does. She sings
in fractured slate.
Haze of breath on a milky bowl.
The crab snaps before knowing
my hands are help,
bringing blood to the tip:
Bright drop. Lost meat.

3. *For the Gatherers*
Combing for membrane, marrow,
remaining tress
at rest in branch and asphalt.
No pieces too small to bless,
to gather and bury.

4. *For Fish*
I loved the smoke-headed birds
hiding gold under tails. Seal-slick,
the boy took my breast
in his mouth. *Do you love it,*
he asked. Hebrew
has no word for like.
The fish persist, unceasing
and unconcerned, an academy of light.
Give me your hand, he said.
Even a smile is a catch
in the flesh. Eye contact is more
water, more light.

Statistics

More good than bad. More blue than black.
More birds than bones. More time than home.
More dogs than horses. More breath than tongue.
More teeth than trees. More blood than wings.
More girl than blood. More light than ice.
More ears. More fingers. More blood
than anything. Less pain than blood.
Less weight than snow. Less silver.
Less care than silence. Less strange
than love. Less love than always.
Less dying than swimming.
More waiting than running.
Less willing than talking.
More eating than asking.
Less drinking than singing.
More burning. Less missing than gone.

After the Tombs (*Tarquinia*)

You are exhuming the distance that connects
your eyes to a lined sheet of paper.
All the symbols of abundance are displayed,

but dry to the touch. You might answer the door
somewhere between the third and seventh knock,
like a bird stopping to bathe in the dust.

Not everyone succumbs to imagination.
When you do, the apricot tree lets down
a single branch distended with fruit.

Nothing else is liquid for miles. The grit
climbing the staircase of your legs tastes of rice
and honey. Only your shoulders think to seek

shelter from the oncoming weather. What good
does it do to wait in stillness, the way
glass waits for disaster?

You Are Not Here

Imperative: second person, future.
(Listen, sweet. Listen. = You will listen. You will.)

*

For my student I write LEAVE LOVE LAUGH.
Not to teach chronology but sound, then tense: I (will) leave.
       You (will) laugh.

*

She left him, I say.
You love him, he says. Repeats. New noise is another thorn
       in the throat. (Laughter.)

*

Today's lesson: Voices that vibrate above the jaw,
that marry tooth to lip. Like feathers, or their opposite.

*

(You are here.
You want to be   *here.)*

*

The role of the verb "to be" always comes loose in the present tense.
In the desert, it dries up. Flies away.

*

See you you will see you will see you soon—

Letters to the Minor Prophet

I'm in Oregon again. The jays
are just as strident here. A flock of juncos

punctuates the garden, dispersing if I speak,
like dandelions spent in a mouthful of air—

*

Your mouth is always part river, part crossing.
We hear the morning light say *reach*,

but too many elevations fall and lift between us,
the country stopping to catch its breath—

*

I'm in Utah. A gull, knee-deep in the canal,
tugs at a sodden, white sock. A pair of avocets

aims for him, screaming—thin plates that slit the air
without shattering. The sock is not a sock,

but another bird, drowned and flayed.
The avocets are praying, if prayer for water birds

means to fling the body at danger again
and again without hitting the ground—

*

I fear punishment for questioning God.
What was it like, your vines picked clean,

fields lost to locusts? I wish we'd met before the fears,
before my name was a cherry pit in the angel's mouth.

But I was a fool, then, too:
always expecting roses—

*

I'm in Oregon now. The world's too wet
for gardening. I want to send you a picture,

a single winged insect. Or do I want to be one,
my hands branching into things that fly?

How to Picture an Edge

Think of an edge like this: You dream your closest
    friend wants to become Catholic. She phones
        to tell you she's just come home from confession—

her second time this week. Your impulse: *rescue*
    her, even if rescue means *meet the edge,*
        and step from your life into hers. She is

the most logical of your friends, immune
    to superstition, even when sanctioned
        in God's name. When you wrote her wedding poem,

you had to find a synonym for prayer,
    so that she wouldn't recognize your call
        to the divine on her behalf. You must

investigate. Like some bumbling sidekick,
    you set out to find whoever
        persuaded her she needed this. You enter

a cathedral, everything Lenten purple—
    the ribbons, the robes dark as arteries.
        You, lacking purple, stand out like the Jew

you are. But this is the edge of the dream:
    Nothing else is changed. She is still the friend
        who had her baby. You are still the friend

who miscarried. This is why her turning
        to unfamiliar faith astonishes
                and even insults you. Even Jews

like you refuse to believe that Jesus
        can make time for the lucky. If her first faith
                was having no faith, and she lost it when

reciting her sins in a curtained booth,
        what hope remains for you, carrying your
                lone heartbeat, no longer speaking to God?

The edge is the line you've drawn between you
        and God, and you guard your anger at Him
                with jealousy. You proceed to the altar.

Good Excuses in Lousy Weather

for Dan

You exhausted the compost of your old vocabulary. You found that the flaw in the absurd was its distance from the finish line, like a circus tent laced shut before the fable's end. On the other hand, you understood the problem with the abstract to be its inability to stop squirrels from raiding the feeder. When you discovered that oenology was a hard science, you decided that drinking wine might have more to teach than previously believed. All morning you had trouble adding up change, offering each cashier your palm of coins as you searched for a second opinion. Two letters arrived from the coast of sleep. One was signed *breathless*. One was signed *soon*. As if there are people in this world who cannot wait to reach you. The letter that never arrived ended like this: *If you ever do anything that stupid, I'll hunt you down in the afterlife and kill you.* The letter that never arrived ended like this: *I'll sink your name with stones.* The letter that never arrived ended like this: *Wait there.*

The Thesaurus Fails to Replace
the Direction of the Sun

You have faced west all your life,
    seeking the spot where God
left the road, conjuring the onset
    of Los Angeles. You embarked
from the epicenter, a place approaching
    algebra in its consistency,
where fields couldn't carry sound.
    (How simple, the wish for water.)
You still face west, praying now
    for nothing to happen, for nothing
to keep happening. These prayers—
    squeezed between wrist
and collarbone—reverse your childhood
    requests for event and mystery,
for something clad in dangerous clothing
    to lay siege to adolescence.
A geographic mishap, like anyone,
    you didn't reflect or reject
the landscape. You stared across
    the horizon's outstretched neck,
blood thrumming to the Burlington Northern,
    attending to the sun's violence
as it hacked trails along the day.
    By the time the light reached you,
you were managing the dark—

not as a bat might,
but like a creature who waits to wake
and head straight to the sea.

In Praise of the Overlooked

1.

(not hands but)

three veins, serpents in transit
to the wrist bone, resembling
Hebrew letters—ones that echo
breath's escape, and warnings
preceding the expired vapor of the patient—

(languages with built-in diphthongs, mimicking blood route and)

mimicking subway maps, the way
lines part, framing
the park, the trick of east to west—

2.

(the arrival bite, vicious, missing the vein to pierce the tendon, my)

doctor of emergencies said
tendons aren't too flamboyant.
Medical terminology
escapes me like sighs, and an animal's tooth,
and years from these veins, and holidays,
the shape they take inside a week
of late snow, mirroring
something unseasonably angry—

3.

(hands weak baskets in the moon's matchlight, not)

        thirty-six years old
and I wanted God's numbers,
the promise of doubled luck. Instead,
faith requires medicine's stiletto,
pinning me in place—

        on my way to the table I was told
which bubbles in the veins
could kill me. How much air
in the tubing the body absorbs—

        (wings.   not wings.)

Excision Sonnets (Pain Scale 0–10)

0.
      one insomniac writes   another:
         make lists   you awake?
            a wall   my mother
thinks   mistake
               left unaddressed
unlabeled envelopes beside the bed:
      stack of emptiness
      letter-writing   invalid
        after her breakdown.   I am
                wrinkled
sheets, Kleenex box?   where to stress "breakdown,"
      syllable in "invalid"? I am
(repeat)   withheld
from view.   like this: life not   .

1.
        a window   look for deer.
      be accurate: I pray for them.
I ask for them.   if they appear
                         won't blame
You any   .   before I lost
             saw a trio
        unclothed   my best
and   enemy (I know
   not Montana,   my car   whole)
        heaviness   make me fight
    see them running   create
a flight   my bones. Until
          I cannot see
them,   It's   late.

2.

    if   deer show up,   God
has gone?   you   silent   long—
        vanishing, unrelated
to biology   faith or deer.)   wrong
  blame the children   winter boots,
            blurred the tracks,   retrace
fresh fire on   edges
of   proof,   gather evidence:
    hard, look hard   pressed itself
       into snow,   history
also. (Missed the turn.)   wiser than prey,
     in   place, following   wolf
In   light.   I'm the one I carry,
       nothing left to   .

3.

Awake   preoccupied
        they returned.   if they're hungry,
if hunger   white-tailed suicide.
(Forget Billings.   angry.
        defeated   crumpled car.)
Why deer?   I   stay in   place
        search   I'd rather
avoid   : *hemorrhage, curettage, trace*
    tissue, necessary.   I
                            explain the body's strange
persistence,   borders   salt,
    unvoiced   I will not lie
                God   arrange
        conception,   *not your fault.*

4.

dangerous to want   so badly.
I   weeks ago. You stayed
   silent   skull.   oddly
half-satisfied   your escape. You fade
    shrinking prison   season,
    bars too small   you   climb   out
    join me.   a reason
for   disappearing.   expected it.
    think I said *come closer?* I meant
   stay away.   *make the body*
fight? I meant   *tight,*   *your life*
a drum   beat,   seal a world. I can't
forgive you this: thinking *daddy.*
I   still cheek-to-   surgeon's knife.

5.

     expelled   whole, but flawed—
        never   grain-of-rice
        picked   names,   always sawed
          (him/her, he/she) always twice-
            open.   prepare
us for fiction? (round.)
    think   math,   a number
      the space it's in. (*if* x) (I found
      blood) (*if* x)   returned
          paraphrase with silence
        call it aphoristic gesture
      through touch, avoid   never learned
 syllables,   oxygen,   science.
Don't ask,   *the curse on me? The*   ?

6.

  ask   this: prayer intercede
      cellular division?   a curse?
        part of me   ready to concede,
           stranger's anger   rehearse
  darker   fruit replacing
fruit (citrus   —I   a grove
below the waist)   missing
        key.   *blighted ov-*
um   serves   doctor's speech
      mouth, inducing   say
    tired   hand
unwanted on my   teach
a thing.   hear *it's nature's way?*
    scale for pain? Point to ten.   beyond.

7.

   stare so   trees,   I could
                          appear, conjure the shape
                        from nothing. Too bad
                             the gap
between   the future. Too bad I
can't conjure   leafless
brush. (Once   a boy   severed my
                             simple as this:

        the brush of a country we
don't belong to.   ) Too
bad   true conjurer.   when
                eyes play tricks   maybe
you   which part comes next. Maybe you
find   a trick.   in vain.

8.

   watch the squirrels   the deer   no-
where   harder to believe
    God when   depends   so
frantic,   say God doesn't leave
                   ?

       give up   deer, seek   divine
      persistent beast,   fat one who
    learned to steal   suet,   upside-down.
           that cage   empty, his
   efforts   vain.   who's to say
      in vain?   who's to say   heals?
(I said   *be ashamed.* Maybe he is.)
   ten-minute operation?   day
          Or   hour with   squirrels?

9.

    can't   January, can't
see it   silent loop, newsreel
                      backward, slow,   won't
    burn   against the lens. Against my will.
      pajamas, television, white
noise   job.   my breakdown in
suburbia.   missing deer. Percoset.
    never answering the   .
           else: dreamed   her. I dream
her still. (never told you   . Never
asked   .) I
dreamed her grown and gone, returned.   seem
     like me   you.   long hair.
And   glad to see   (You know why.)

10.
                play it (paint it?)   reverse,
get her to grow?   watch too much
TV,   medicine. Spring's worse,
     snow   aquifer, can't watch
     deer,   ambush God.   find
an archaeologist   dig   out,
     excavate   eras long (rewind?
                preserve   I'll forget.
     if—   up, tunneling down—
          my double,   ask her
     if   life   reverse,   can go
to   start, how do you measure pain?
          hurt (aching? stabbing?)   *gesture*
replacing speech, point to ten? Or zero?

The Alphabet of Claudia

Afterlife

doesn't think about animals   ignores the soft beasts
pressing on her ankles—
                knows how to read a twisted tongue—
speaks in warped aphorism:
  it's the unimportant truths that obscure the important lie
doesn't remember the Pacific

                           wet pressure
                      permanent exhale
knows the names of mountains but won't recall other
        elevations

                where air divides itself in two
                saves itself for no one
remembers the Mediterranean

                 zipped-up bricks
                  the last address
        in her insulated, untranslated skin.

Any Way

What does she mean by *bottle glass*?
                              The kind that redistributes light.
What does she mean by *hysteria*?
                              Every night and every day.
What does she mean by *carry on*?
                              Held too tight. Breaking.

Appearance

hears her eyes are sky blue
hears she is unexpected
        makes the mistake of saying a short prayer.
                        (*azul*)
                waits to be translated.
                    (*inesperada*)

Astronomy

She means to see the Perseids
                      bright windfalls collected in her skirts
but the hour
                                          so late
the safety net
                                          so thin
the stars
                                      too close
    immolation begins
        oh, querido mio, how they stitched the sky
                          with a single spark.

Catalogue

oil spills
falling

encountering the enemy unexpectedly
the weight of water on her unprepared bones

the segue into nothingness—
She measures, for the first time, the dimensions of the word *need:*
a room with white corners
a ball of yarn like endless weeping

what should I do now?

City

She collects the sounds that marry the story:

the O, O, O
for the highwire walker

the I, I, I—

Definitions (*Mistake*)

thinking it helps to see disaster approaching

thinking history bothers to knock

(the third has no alphabet)

Exile

for *I am so far from my country.*

Future

See the mirror on the other side of October
                              reflecting the emptiness
                                   in her feet
                    an impression like the back of a scar

the interior of a smile
the converse of the airplane's trajectory
                                   crossing the equator.

North

She is driving.

from bad weather to worse.

keeps the habit: one hand on her belly.

nothing is right

On her right a red truck issues a license plate command:

4GIVE

the room is nearly emptied

Three hundred more miles and she is circled.

in a single thought.

one question for the heaven of bumper stickers:

who can I forgive?

who can I forgive?

Patriarch

looking for a hole in the law

                                        knotsized, for peeking

        She carries her troubles like a loonmother
carried her grandfather

                                    once he could sing

now he is ground for placing stones
        considers him all the time

                                    would he be angry

she places stones

                                    would he be angry

    chunks   nothing   the weight of the atmosphere
Somewhere, the father of her child reaches for a telephone—

          So many disasters encroach when you're alone.

Queries

She wonders

does *minimal*
mean *irreducible*?
(is the minimum ever sufficient?)
might *sufficient*
mean only *a wolf's tooth, dropped in a gutter of light*?

Southern Cross

She won't   resort to mourning

                  red dust

        we are far from home

                 penguins
                 tus pajaros

                 beaches
                 tu arena

          his tongue on the black road
                 mi lengua

              as they drove west
   better to seek trouble than to let trouble track you down

gives away her lines
         her lights
           all the lightyears to heaven
                   for a footnote—

Untitled

Claudia goes to a party

her hands

in his pockets

she steals

his red sunglasses

they stand

please,
hemisphere to

hemisphere

have some

wine

look—

these are not the same

stars

not my

tell me

stars
your name.

Waiting

double-shelled,
    Brunelleschi's dome,
        all spiral and helix and *feats of engineering*—

                        She is outnumbered
her heart leaps to her mouth
where her tongue cleaves unwanted guests
and her teeth hide silent under her tongue

                        small ash secrets
                            sleeping stars
                 weeks of impatience.

Wake

Claudia tries to see all the way to heaven

                                        reaching only the contrails

crossing God's eyes

              but what is heaven without bourbon?

                           reaching only the ether holding us in

       the worst thing about the present is its repetitive nature

holding us in

                      We are living in the afterlife—

LISTEN, SWIMMER

Seventeen Lessons About Utopia

1. *Gesture*
We don't disclose the signal of this utopia: internal shrug crossed
with visible smile.

2. *Narcotics*
Caffeine, codeine, Percoset. The house in its hour before sleep.

  Can you describe the difference between "mask" and "analgesic"?

3. *Meteorology*
Weather permitted, we'd go naked all the time, but our
perceptions aren't that temperate. The climate is sentient and
obeys desire. The wind, in her fondness for gallant gestures,
blows in four-part harmony.
  Pay attention. Define "tropical depression." Is it a sigh? A size?
  Terminal, or treatable?

4. *Biochemistry*
Blood hits the air dry like unwatered marigolds, dark as mums
under frost.

5. *My Language*
It stutters, starts, bends itself to the body's orders. It ties in the
back, an apron of muslin and muffled inquiry.

6. *Finance*
Our currency is persistence and supplication: the twin dogs of faith.

7. *Etymology*
Words we love but avoid: *ache, angel, heart, sorrow.*

Words we collect in secret: *crabtrap, filigree, ironwork, sylvanshine.*

> *Memorize new parts of speech by holding them hostage under your gums. Sear your vernacular into the skin: lozenges of ash.*

We gather words that shape seasons. Time-and-place, turning earth: *Diurnal, heliotropic. Wax* and *wane.*
Front, equinox.
Constellate.

We enforce the names of fishes that evoke the breathing creatures: *clownfish, lionfish, parrotfish, sea star.*

8. *Anthropology*
We decorate in splendor and opulence. We frame our features in jeweled windows. Light enters dyed bright and can't leave.

> *Where does reflection begin the journey it takes to find your face?*

9. *Religion*
The worst sin is the tattoo. We are painted, we are engraved, we are scarred and emblazoned. We get lazy, touching each other's tattoos and calling it prayer.

What is heresy? Empty-handedness, forgetting to wake up early, forgetting to forsake sleep.

10. *Work*
We make our living documenting the science of losing
consciousness. We recite dreams from memory, from the
moment we wake up until the moment we reach for the lens.

*First, recite the dream you just tripped over. The receding one, the
one shrinking from your waking mouth. Then the night before
that. And the night before that, until you are curled in seaweed
and parable, asleep before reminiscence.*

11. *Legerdemain*
We practice invisibility, higher visibility, blindness in clear
light, and insight in fog.

12. *The Argument of Art and Science*
We want to debunk the myth of snowflakes.

13. *Cartography*
We name our geography to invoke the places we have been,
small memorials to danger and grace, to the limbs we've
retained, to the famine we've been lucky to flee. Here, a hot
corner in Trastevere, or is it Tiberias? Is it the Sinai, or just a
footbridge, some bad clams, a cobbled alley where the moon's
tooth sequesters its light?

*For weeks you dreamed you were on your way out of this country,
even after your arrival. Now for the first, second, even third time
you're dreaming you've gone back.*

14. *Medicine*
Our physicians are spiders, treating us with eight-legged silence
and silk, distributing composure and endurance in their free
clinics.

15. *A Legislature of Animals*
The rulers of this utopia are the jesters and the clowns. They
tool around on unicycles, juggling flame. Small, furred animals
dart about. We have guinea fowl, peacocks, egrets, and geese.
We don't debate euthanasia.

> *Who was so lazy when they named you, fish? Couldn't you have*
> *a shape, a consistency all to yourself? Instead we see you and we*
> *think parrot, we think lion, we think angel or clown. As if the*
> *land and the sky and all of their children came first, when*
> *in fact it was the water who first parted herself for the earth.*

Insects are turned back at the border.

16. *Reproduction*

> *After we fuck you come back into yourself the way you return to*
> *earth when the plane lands. Then, the overstock of gratitude—*
> *breath expelled, wheels to tarmac, limbs to limbs to sheets. You are*
> *halfway sitting up before you know it. "Is this you leaving?"*
> *This is me leaving.*

We are hot milk sipped after the battlefield of our names.

17. *Sin*
In this utopia we have an angry grip on the illicit.

The bottom of our river is pure.

TABLOIDS

(This is for the clown who sweeps up the world at the end of the night.)

UNCOMFORTABLE OBJECT DISCOVERED IN DOCTOR'S OFFICE.
The medievalists like to get together after hours and make toys for
children . . . leaving a wake, a runway, a way to speak to aliens—

GIANT PHONE BOOTHS DEVELOP TASTE FOR HUMAN FLESH.
In Bolivia, I was tall.
Step.   Step.

CITY PLANNER LOCKED IN ATTIC EATS HIS OWN HANDS.
I am trying to save Manhattan.
No light, no water, no earth, no—

ALIENS LAND AT SORORITY PICNIC.
Shhhhh—

NOTHING REMAINS, FILM AT 11.
Dante said very little on his deathbed—
Botticelli would have painted the entire Divine Comedy
had he lived—

The monks traveled so slowly they stopped.

The Jews bury paper if it carries God's name—

Underwater

The first time the other life was leaving, or leaking,
we were sinking in the cup of our pact:
Keep the babies safe by remaining unmade.
Rules for moving the injured are strict.

We were sinking in the cup of our pact:
Keep them strapped to something inanimate.
Rules for moving the injured are strict.
Rules for moving the dead are less.

Keep them strapped to something inanimate
the way we keep gravity strapped to our feet.
Rules for moving the dead are less
like a grip stripped of sanity—

the way we keep gravity strapped to our feet
as waves wait to escape the grasp of the shore
like a grip stripped of sanity—
Swimmer at the soul's coastline,

as waves wait to escape the grasp of the shore.
You found the fjords and hollowed their wholes.
Swimmer at the soul's coastline,
blinking the ink from maps of the eye,

you found the fjords and hollowed their wholes.
(Why is the price of everything this eternal vigilance?)
Blinking the ink from maps of the eye,
I only wanted to be to you as sand to glass:

(Why is the price of everything this eternal vigilance?)
You believed that I meant *indispensable*.
I only wanted to be to you as sand to glass:
I meant *raw, sifted, on the verge of liquid*.

You believed that I meant *indispensable*
the first time the other life was leaving, or leaking.
I meant *raw, sifted, on the verge of liquid*.
Keep the babies safe by remaining unmade.

Letter from the Editor

Listen, swimmer, the past is always on my left. Just don't stand there. Does everything come down to capitulation or resistance? Last night I had a dream about the scar on my left hand, where the cleaver ended its flight, leaving a letter, a little hook of language. Swimmer, listen. Pull these leaves and branches from my tongue. Just don't let them lie there because you made them grow. About your fear of sunken things: Is it the density or the dimension? Is it the thought of all that water, the transparent weight pressing the dead ship into the ocean floor and sealing it there, like a body sealed against another body on an August day too hot for sex—

Epithalamium (in seven disciplines)

1. *Cosmochronology (the science of the age of stars)*
Before I knew you, I spent half my life below the surface, coming up for air only when the sun reached melancholy in the slatted sky. Before you knew me I was only texture: velvet, sandpaper, and gooseflesh. Before I knew you I was a rain gauge at midsummer. A camp stove during the burning season. Before you knew me, you hid your unstrung heart in the snow and fashioned winter boots from the skins of a dozen supernovae so that your feet might light a path home over the cobblestones of the soul's slick alleyways.

2. *Catacoustics (of echoes)*
I was always looking for the ricochet of your reflection in a pool of polished stone. You were always waiting for my voice in the trace of light that scars the wet sky.

3. *Pharology (of lighthouses)*
When we were not invented I strapped a camera to my forehead and walked backward into an evening sea, daring the local phosphorescence to construct someone I could really talk to from the breath of high tide. When we were not invented you tied a listening dish to the roof and tried to transcribe the invisible music of bats. When we were not invented we stood back to back where water and sand join hands and asked the whole continent to bend so that we could stand face to face.

4. *Sphygmology (of the pulse)*
Once someone told us that it was unnatural to say "I love you" in Chinese. But I do love you in Chinese. I love you in Chinese, in English, in semaphore and in smoke signal and in telegraph. I love you via satellite and I love you during the delay on the line that represents the earth's curve. I love you in the shape of X. I love you in the presence of light. I love you when the light is fading behind you.

5. *Proxemics (of the human need for personal space)*
The verge of joy is also its own kind of happiness.

6. *Pteryology (of the distribution of feathers on birds)*
Once I was all quill and barb, plume and spike, carrying useless aerodynamics on my back and waiting. Now I know that every wing has a history, a memory of the first journey through the air, pushing against nothing until nothing becomes solid. Now I know wings are no longer wounds but maps we tattoo on the bellies of clouds.

7. *Thaumatology (of miracles and wonders)*
Before the science of you, cardiology was only an empty box at the back of the closet. Meteorology was a wet afternoon in a chilly room. Cosmology was beauty school for the Milky Way.

A Meteorologist in the Promised Land

The linguistics of clouds changes from country to country.
What connotes a storm at home is only a child's flushed cheek

pressed close to the tropical atmosphere.
New climates can render me illiterate.

What began as relief turned to sunburn,
like the voice of the man next door,

soft in the sky's throat, but treacherous.
When we touch I'm struck

by the paleness of his nailbeds in his brown fingertips
against the reddened error of my skin.

Signals for disaster here are only another kind of silence:
the sea holding its breath, a lover's hands gone too still.

Misreading the air, I'm caught without my umbrella,
the shibboleth staining my shoes with mud,

rinsing me clean with rainwater.
This country keeps infinite grammars of betrayal, beginning

with syllables of shadow appearing beneath my fingers,
mispronounced as the fog burns away.

THE WAR IN THE NORTH: A REPORT

Prologue (July 2006)

This is not the piece called *Aftermath*, or the piece called *We Were Right and You Were Wrong*. This is not the piece called *Omen of Things Falling into the Sea*. This is the piece called *The Rest of the Body Waits, Awake*. I'd like a better word for waiting, but *attend* is too expectant and *expect* is too smug.

1. We Are Perfectly Safe in Jaffa (Daytime)

Later that same day we find ourselves on the beach, the best place for watching the helicopters, unless you don't want to see the heavy artillery slung below their bellies like sharp-edged lamprey nearly ready to drop off and find another shark's guts to vacuum. Children whine in the sand. Some of their mothers are between cigarettes; some of their mothers are between geographies, always knowing that the words *compass*, *conscience*, and *north* are related. These mothers drop their cigarettes in the surf and wait with the patience of the dead to retrieve their children from the waves. These mothers are the color of butter, the color of turtle beans, the color of Sabbath wax. The color of Jerusalem stone. The color of dirt in Missouri.

2. We Are Perfectly Safe in Jaffa (Evening)

They said the service at the Sea Bar left something to be desired. What they meant was that their desire was still intact at the end of the evening's reach. As always they were having trouble expressing time, despite the density of their vocabularies. I would have shown them where to go had they bothered to ask, but bothering and asking are two chapters in two books that sit in flagrant friction on the same shelf. In a country where nothing is forbidden, everything forbidden begins to look sacred.

3. Insomnia

I go outside without binoculars because I no longer trust anything translucent to suffer my gravity. Up and to the west appear the midnight sorties like fireflies in search of an exorcist. Like last night's phone call, a creature so miserable it should have its own museum. Does yesterday count as today if I spent the night half vertical, one-quarter sedated and thirty-three-percent occupied by mosquitoes? Silence must be incursive to exist here, a string in the ear pulled tight to make a small purse.

4. Walking in Tel Aviv (West To East)

The graffiti says, *Blessed is the Lord, I am suffering.* Or perhaps, *Blessed is the Lord, I suffer.* (More so than yours, mine is a language of implication.) *Blessed is the Lord, I suffer. Blessed is the Lord, I am suffering.* From *suffer* comes the word *patient*, which says more about the locker rooms of language and faith than I can cram onto the head of a camel. *Blessed is the Lord, I am patient.*

5. Family

The call from my cousin snaps like a rattlesnake. *We can't talk about where he's stationed.* His son is on maneuvers near the butterfly bush, not the spot for folding antennae in heat-sponsored bliss. *Not on a cell phone.* His wings are the family pride; I am just another failed biped wiping my feathers from ledges. *But he's OK for now.*

6. Language Lesson

In Hebrew I'm more than a signal fire in this ocean of grief in Hebrew the gun runners follow my orders in Hebrew the wind comes straight from the desert, strong enough to disassemble God's snores in Hebrew the words for "cherry" and "clitoris" sound pleasingly similar in Hebrew I'm the proper kind of beautiful in Hebrew there's a word for the day before yesterday and a day for the word before that in Hebrew the fish are less than nameless and more than anonymous in Hebrew the men downstairs will talk about my breasts in Hebrew superstitions blow in from the west like the fruit vendors' voices in Hebrew—

7. Reported on the News (I)

This is the sea, relentless and blind in midmorning tides, stubborn surfers, and migratory terns. This is the television screen, approximately the same shape and size as the train window, from which they gathered ground glass and hung sirens from the ceilings in bright streamers. I know these men with their bright vests already, more meticulous and faithful than vultures, growing the same lousy stares with which to assess the spread.

8. A Vocabulary

I know the difference between arsenal and artery, weapon and wedge, lever and lover. Do you want to know how many helicopters have passed since I began to stain this day into the leaf and breath that make a page? A formation's worth, a day's worth. I know the difference between battery and brushoff. Between reckless endangerment and restless endearment. Between your hollow talisman and what you killed to build it.

9. Reported on the News (II)

Upon hearing that the rockets made it all the way to Ashkelon, I remember the summer I was ten: tidepools and the words inside them, starfish and salt air, picnics and pickled garlic. A bulbul's serenade: Such a complicated thought for such a small bird. *Six notes and silence, six notes and silence.*

10. Rumor

Do you remember the shooting in the square? I only recall the cats there and the lady trees that left fat inedible fruit on every surface. A garden gone wrong. But gunfire could have been anywhere in the tentacles of a gentle society turned animal-skin out, turned clawfoot upsidedown. The trees weren't broken, just mateless and weeping with fruit, too insensate to remember a murder. Maybe I was sleeping.

11. In Case of Emergency

In my dream I comforted the souls of the curious, who had wandered too close to the Katyushas. (That part is true.) When the floods come, the righteous will all be given lanterns. Or mercury flashlights. The bulletins are broadcast at one o'clock, then at four o'clock, then for the last time at seven. The shiny brochure they shoved under the door says this: *Remember: unusual reactions are natural in an emergency situation.* July was only minutes ago.

12. Two Days As The Artist's Model (An Intermission)

She holds the painting to a mirror to see where she's erred. When asked if I know this technique I admit I've practiced it my whole life. A portraitist is an odd kind of fortune teller; she understands where bone and skin must be cut for the rest of the body to breathe. Her candles go unlit but still sell light. Even here I sense a song amid the sirens, two words translated from Hebrew: *I'm afraid, I'm afraid.*

13. Dream Journal: Asleep in a Bombproof Room

I am torn between attending the dinner for the whores and the memorial for Anne Frank. The whores call to confirm but I end up eating for Anne instead—cold lasagna and garlic bread. All I wanted was the crust. I wake up wondering what side of the building I'll land on when the Katyushas come . . . I had spices in my mouth and too much to carry. We were meant to catch what fell to the table. The man hadn't touched me but neither had he gained entry in the legal way. I left when I saw the backs of his arms, which reminded me of June rain. The wall was all asylum and my hand began to write itself. Brother, we must have had a swimming lesson on the same day in different pools. When you learned to hold your breath I peeked and nothing has fit properly since. *In the kingdom of the blind . . .* We were kissing with our mouths full of sand. . . . *the one-eyed man is still one-eyed.* Lately I've become obsessed with dimension.

14. Walking in Tel Aviv (South to North)

The artillery of midmorning sunlight excises clouds and leaves bone blue behind, a precise technique meant to scatter rebellious weather fomenting in cumulonimbus troops massing on the horizon's spine. Of course I went to the ocean: it's the only border I can spend the day crossing unarmed. At some point in the history of every day I start to list, as if the day were the sea and I the bad boat with dented hull and snapped keel. At some point in the day I reach out, and I'm righted. Yesterday I saw a man carrying a turkey by the wingtips. The skin on its head was bluish, like held breath. The man stood arguing with two other men, which is to say conversing. The turkey moved its mouth but made no sounds. And looked around. And then hung still in its cold flight. As if to say, *Only the brainless are patient.*

15. One Way to Talk About the Helicopters

The helicopter's shadow swings straps over the forgotten bathmat of flies we call a beach. The letter you sent carries a coast's wish and thumbprints of twenty time zones, as if lost sleep is merely a handful of unredeemed raffle tickets. The single time we were underwater together we visited different seas. I hold my breath until the next one. And the next.

16. Creation Myth

We were told the story of Babel because the city was half-finished. What flooded through there, what plagued the brickmakers and the brickburners as they ritualized the straw-beating, the mud-pulling, the shaping and molding and matting and patting? Before the rains came, did they run home to beat their children and make love to their slaves? Did they stop at the 7–11 in the middle of the storm to grab a pack of matches and a Slim Jim? When did the people scatter like misunderstood geraniums after the first frost, dropping their petals in formless accusation? Only later, at the hands of the redactors, did Babel become a story of God's anger. Latest of all was the erasure of God's caprice, designed to block the last recesses of the imagination's keep, where we curl in a granite cave cold with moss and sweat.

17. Another Way to Talk About the Helicopters

Yesterday they took a shortcut over the city, seam-rippers pulling at the extra threads of our routine. The helicopters corrupt history, tearing the city's hem like my crazed aunties busy with their sewing kits. Pinned against sunset they are almost beautiful, a trick of the dark pointing west.

18. Anatomy Lesson

The prophets boil bones for soup, rendered from the flesh, which was rendered from the bull, which was rendered from life with a hatchet and a knife. Are two instruments of rendition overkill or ordinary? Rend. Render. I rendered those words from the flesh of their language. Like the Spanish Inquisition. *Converso, reverso, morisco, marrano.* A knock at the door, flawless and fatal. *We're here for your rendering.* From faith to faith. From the fat we render tallow, a wax for lighting the way. Then soup bones, Jew bones. All bones begin as a gathering of calcium prescribed by code. All renderings begin as a way of explication, which is not to say explanation, for which reason might have to prevail.

19. Yet Another Way

We abandoned our best behavior long ago. We took up arms to protect the stones. To protect the light, to occupy the sun, to lasso sparked waves with the tongues of helicopter blades, those faded angels who strip the sleep from darkness. We make too much machinery. We pretend helicopters are eagles. We pretend bullets are our own invention.

20. The Doubled Burden of Biblical Grammar

In the kingdom of transitive verbs, "disappear" is the joker, the jester, the clown. The thief, the usurper, the pretender. The sacrificial ram. The sacrificial knife at the quivering throat of the sacrificial ram. The untrembling hand holding the sacrificial knife to the quivering throat of the sacrificial ram. The angel in the tree who commands the hand to stop. The wings of the angel in the tree, with their clotted feathers and odd stench in the off season. In the kingdom of transitive verbs, "disappear" is the hired gun, the king's doublecrossing assassin, the staff Moses throws to the ground and turns into a snake to scare the Pharaoh into a new belief system. "Disappear" is the Pharaoh's untrained, unconcerned gaze, still weeks before he will kneel at the bedside of his son's unmoving body and curse the God of the Jews, and curse the Jews.

21. Ceasefire

Blood has its own syntax. Let me send you a draft of this tissue-thin grip we have on breathing. Say what you came to say, quick before the helicopters wake up and remind the rockets where to drop, before trouble presses new shapes into your sleeping brain and waits for you to fling your eyes apart in a panic.

Epilogue (August)

It's the hoopoe I miss first, with his fan-handed head and flighty mate. And the walk through the park that took me to him, the iron gate meant to prevent something I never discerned. And the one-way traffic in the skinny street, and the tiled doors that surrendered to it. And the dogs with their balls and the guards with their wands. But first I miss the hoopoe, and then the bulbuls, with their secret splash of yellow feathers and their joyful throats, with their many words that stay just out of my grasp, like whisperers in the last seat of a train gazing so intensely they supplant language. I miss the hoopoes and the bulbuls. I miss the boy who made my coffee and that particularly dusty stretch of a Jaffa street where, with an ocean of breath, an armful of concrete went sliding through the plastic sleeve, a six-story drop into a dumpster filled with oblivion.

Notes & Acknowledgements

'T'Philot' is the Hebrew word for prayers. (Hebrew does, of course, have a word for *like*.)

'Epithalamium' is for Emily and Brian Goedde.

'Letter from the Editor' is for Jason Grunebaum.

'Statistics' came from a performance piece that Jason Grunebaum and I created based on the writing we exchange daily. For this writing, for your friendship, and for putting a roof over my head when I needed it, I am ever thankful, and remarkably lucky.

Thank you to Robin Hemley and the participants of the 2007 Overseas Writing Workshop for their help with 'The War in the North.'

Thank you also to Brian Booker for his fantastic art and Tony Frazer for taking a chance on me.

Finally, the following people gave their encouragement, advice, and time, for which I am eternally grateful. Without them this book would not exist: Erin Malone, Christopher Merrill, Idra Novey, Brenda Shaw, Cole Swensen, and Diana Thow. Russell Valentino deserves special mention for keeping me on track in other matters.

www.ingramcontent.com/pod-product-compliance
Lightning Source LLC
Chambersburg PA
CBHW031928080426
42734CB00007B/603